THE DOG WHO HAS PEOPLE BARKING
WITH LAUGHTER . . .

Whether he's patrolling the neighborhood and minding every-one's business or bringing home somebody's brand-new hat, offering a bone to a hungry friend or scrounging a meal from his favorite kids, Marmaduke's always on the prowl for fun and frolic. Syndicated in hundreds of newspapers around the globe, he's become the beloved buddy of dog fanciers every-where, and now he's here to share his hilarious adventures with you.

MEET MARMADUKE!

More Big Laughs from SIGNET

☐ **ZIGGY FACES LIFE by Tom Wilson.** (114280—$1.75)
☐ **THIS BOOK IS FOR THE BIRDS by Tom Wilson.**
(119606—$1.75)
☐ **IT'S A ZIGGY WORLD by Tom Wilson.** (119681—$1.75)
☐ **LIFE IS JUST A BUNCH OF ZIGGYS by Tom Wilson.**
(119924—$1.75)
☐ **ZIGGYS OF THE WORLD UNITE! by Tom Wilson.**
(112717—$1.50)
☐ **PLANTS ARE SOME OF MY FAVORITE PEOPLE by Tom Wilson.**
(121619—$1.75)
☐ **PETS ARE FRIENDS YOU LIKE WHO LIKE YOU RIGHT BACK by Tom Wilson.** (115783—$1.50)
☐ **NEVER GET TOO PERSONALLY INVOLVED IN YOUR OWN LIFE by Tom Wilson.** (119843—$1.75)
☐ **ZIGGY FACES LIFE . . . AGAIN! by Tom Wilson.**
(117905—$1.95)*
☐ **HIP KIDS' LETTERS FROM CAMP by Bill Adler.**
(071077—95¢)
☐ **MORE LETTERS FROM CAMP by Bill Adler.** (085809—$1.25)
☐ **STILL MORE LETTERS FROM CAMP by Bill Adler.**
(089464—$1.25)

*Price slightly higher in Canada

Buy them at your local bookstore or use this convenient coupon for ordering.

THE NEW AMERICAN LIBRARY, INC.,
P.O. Box 999, Bergenfield, New Jersey 07621

Please send me the books I have checked above. I am enclosing $_____
(please add $1.00 to this order to cover postage and handling). Send check
or money order—no cash or C.O.D.'s. Prices and numbers are subject to change
without notice.

Name_____

Address_____

City _____ State _____ Zip Code _____
Allow 4-6 weeks for delivery.
This offer is subject to withdrawal without notice.

MEET MARMADUKE®!

By
Brad Anderson

A SIGNET BOOK

NEW AMERICAN LIBRARY

TIMES MIRROR

SIGNET TRADEMARK REG. U.S. PAT. OFF. AND FOREIGN COUNTRIES
REGISTERED TRADEMARK—MARCA REGISTRADA
HECHO EN CHICAGO, U.S.A.

SIGNET, SIGNET CLASSICS, MENTOR, PLUME, MERIDIAN AND
NAL BOOKS are published by The New American Library, Inc.,
1633 Broadway, New York, New York 10019

First Printing, March, 1983

1 2 3 4 5 6 7 8 9

PRINTED IN THE UNITED STATES OF AMERICA

"Is this the bone you've been looking for?"

1-5-82 © 1981 United Feature Syndicate, Inc.

"I learned how to tie bows today!"

"Will you get out of here, Marmaduke...I
almost unscrewed your nose!"

"Off! And never mind that 'why don't you
sit in the kitchen' look!"

1-8-82   © 1981 United Feature Syndicate, Inc.

"You forgot to say goodbye to him."

1-9-82 © 1981 United Feature Syndicate, Inc. BRAD ANDERSON

"Sometimes Marmaduke hides his bubble
gum behind his ear, Aunt Shirley."

"Move over! I've read this page three times
and still don't know what it says!"

"Does a large Great Dane live here?"

"Hold your fire! It's Marmaduke
with a convoy!"

"Maybe fish don't like to eat bones,
Marmaduke."

"...And no flipping the light switch off!"

"A cat ran across the TV screen."

"I suggest you stay in your doghouse
until Dottie gets over your eating
up her casserole!"

"Let him in. I'd rather he came through
the door than the window."

1·20   © 1982 United Feature Syndicate, Inc.   BRAD ANDERSON

"Hold it, you two...I'LL set the thermostat!"

1-21   © 1982 United Feature Syndicate, Inc.

"We're playing beautician..."

"We made a deal...if I pull him around the block, he'll let me sit in my new easy chair."

"So THAT'S where our electric blanket was!"

"It's nice you think so much of me,
but I can't drive like this!"

"Thank goodness for remote control."

"The interest rate will be
18%...17%...16...how about a flat 10%?!"

"He knows what laps are for."

"You'd better hurry! Marmaduke wants to
see the dog cartoons!"

"Bad news, Casanova!"

"I don't want to wake him, either...but
we HAVE to answer that robbery-in-progress."

"Don't expect any help from me...
I'm in the doghouse myself!"

"You wanted something?"

"I'd better start shoveling."

"Can't you wait until I'm out of the house
before you crawl in there?"

"Don't bother checking the TV Log...
we only have one choice...dog cartoons."

"You're forgetting something.
I'M the boss!"

"We raffled you off, Marmaduke, but you know how to find your way home again."

"SPOILSPORT!"

"Three chocolate sodas, please...
one in a bowl!"

"I didn't know we were having breakfast in bed this morning."

"You might as well turn the motor off...
you know how expensive gas is!"

"Has anybody seen my winter hat
and sheepskin coat?"

"So?...I have bony knees!"

"Maybe if you got home at a decent hour,
they wouldn't lock you out!"

"No wonder we couldn't sleep!"

2·19

© 1982 United Feature Syndicate, Inc.

© 1982 United Feature Syndicate, Inc.

"I take it you're postponing your trip
until spring."

"I can't explain it...whenever he barks,
the automatic garage door opens!"

2·23 © 1982 United Feature Syndicate, Inc.

"When will you learn that
neatness counts?!"

"That's only the foothill...wait till it
gets to the mountains!"

"I don't know what you've done this time,
but that disguise won't fool anyone!"

2·26 ©1982 United Feature Syndicate, Inc.

"Marmaduke just LOVES grandmas!"

"Phil! Discipline him!"

© 1982 United Feature Syndicate, Inc.

3-1

"Mom, I wish you wouldn't send Duke
for me in front of the guys!"

3-2

"It's the equivalent of a doggie bag
from the finest restaurant in town!"

"If you hit Marmaduke with a snowball,
he hits you with a BLIZZARD!"

3-4

"Honest, Marmaduke, you're the only
dog in my life."

"There...I've solved the mystery
of the snoring coats!"

"Don't be impatient...you'll get your
gingerbread dog soon."

"You're right...they're not very good!"

"We never disagree which way to go.
He goes his way and I go with him."

"You're a '10,' Marmaduke, a real '10.'"

"You'll never be fully paid for!"

"Tell him the next time my hat blows off,
to let it blow!"

"Watch him regain the will to live."

"See? The birds like him because
he protects them!"

"Can't it wait until later? I'm too tired
to play King Solomon!"

"It isn't hungry! It just wants a drink!"

BRAD ANDERSON   3-17

"Well, I'll be! Where did Marmaduke learn
the secret handshake of the
Order of Eastern Mystics?!"

"It's your fault. You thought I had
plenty of room!"

"Mom, he wants peanut butter and jelly
on his bone!"

3-22 © 1982 United Feature Syndicate, Inc. BRAD ANDERSON

"Marmaduke wants to keep an eye
on the neighborhood!"

."Is this the only place where they can
come in out of the cold?"

SLURP!

© 1982 United Feature Syndicate, Inc.

3·24

"Why can't we just be pals?!"

"I wonder what the reigning monarch
wants us to do today?"

3-25 © 1982 United Feature Syndicate, Inc. BRAD ANDERSON

© 1982 United Feature Syndicate, Inc.

3-26

"Stop chasing the birds with that
feeder...they'll find it on their own!"

"Just when I got rid of that last batch
of hats, we have another windy day!"

3-29   BRAD ANDERSON

"Not that chair, Mrs. Marsh...
it's Marmaduke's!"

"It's the animal shelter. Did you chase their
dogcatcher out of town?"

3-30 © 1982 United Feature Syndicate, Inc.

"May Fred look around? He's missing a
NO TRESPASSING sign."

"Whew! What he needs is a good dose of
spring fever!"

"He's no trouble. He does what he wants, and we do what he wants."

"Guess what we spring clean next?!"

© 1982 United Feature Syndicate, Inc.

4.3

"Never mind that cross-your-heart trick...
a beef patty is missing, and you're
the prime suspect!"

© 1962 United Feature Syndicate, Inc.

"Wake up! Tell me this is only a nightmare!"

"May I have that remote control? I'm tired
of dog food commercials."

"Marmaduke's ready for his grapefruit."

"He's ASKING us to put him in there...
I smell a mass escape plan!"

"He doesn't get up unless it's something worthwhile."

"Marmaduke learned one thing in Sunday school yesterday...to love his neighbor!"

4·20 © 1982 United Feature Syndicate, Inc.

"Am I getting all this attention because you love me, or because the kids are in school?"

© 1982 United Feature Syndicate, Inc.

"Who set the blanket on high?"

4.22 BRAD ANDERSON

"He hid his bones in the 'old clothes' closet
and they all smell of mothballs!"

"Don't you ever WALK home?"

"Better shake hands with him...it's a
new trick he just learned!"

4-24 © 1982 United Feature Syndicate, Inc.

"Marmaduke is helping the early birds
find a worm!"

4-27 © 1982 United Feature Syndicate, Inc.

"Marmaduke gets upset if anyone talks
during a dog food commercial."

4·28 © 1982 United Feature Syndicate, Inc. BRAD ANDERSON

"Marmaduke's letting them stay with him
until they find a place of their own!"

4-29

"Don't you even feel a *twinge* of guilt?"

"I'm sorry...I didn't know you don't like
cigar smoke in the house!"

"Do you still think you haven't
spoiled him?"

"He hides them every trash pickup day!"

"Stop! Stop! No kisses while I'm working!"

5·5

"See what happens when you sleep out
in the bushes."

"He's not trying to catch his tail...
he's looking for the designer label on
his new sweater."

"I warn you...Marmaduke wants you to get up!"

5-8 © 1982 United Feature Syndicate, Inc.

"Every time they scold you, you come over
here and give me that ol' buddy stuff."

"I gotta think of something that will
make Dottie mad enough to put me
in the doghouse."

"Hold the gossip until I get rid of ol'
MR. BIG EARS!"

"Brother Marmaduke has just proposed a
sun roof for our clubhouse!"

"You won't believe this, but I was dragged
six miles in the marathon race and
won third place!"

"Well, so much for the old 'get your
foot in the door' theory!"

"No wonder we can't go! You tied
Marmaduke to the bumper!"

"I'm worried! He's taking the punishment
before I discover the crime!"

5·18   BRAD ANDERSON

"Won't he ever forget about you turning
the hose on him?"

"IGNORE him...I'll do the ordering!"

"Don't get your hopes up Zsa Zsa...
he smells this roast from the oven."

5·20   © 1982 United Feature Syndicate, Inc.

"We're going to the vet...maybe!"

5·22   BRAD ANDERSON

"Sure you carried him to his bed when he was a puppy...but now he's spoiled rotten."

5-26   © 1982 United Feature Syndicate, Inc.

"Hey, I'm *not* Phil...I'm fragile."

"You wouldn't look so great either if you had been at the lodge meeting last night."

"Mrs. Winslow! Our little Mitsy has a
visitor. Would you care to know the rest?"

5·24

"In case you didn't know, hammocks were
not meant to be jumped on!"

"I'll toss you to see who shares the bed
with him and who gets the sofa!"

5.29 © 1982 United Feature Syndicate, Inc.

"Hey, Mom! Look what followed
Marmaduke home!"

© 1982 United Feature Syndicate, Inc.

POLICE

"He wants a ride home...ignore him!"

"And here are your after-dinner mints."

"He loves being petted, but if you stop,
WATCH OUT!"

"I don't blame him...it scares me, too!"